Inklings Book 2009

I0157673

Grateful acknowledgment is made to the following young authors for contributing their poems and short stories.

Caleb Adderley
Amrita Bhasin
Suah Cheong
Natalie Gould
Meg Maurer
Kaitlyn Penchina
Kit Sanderson
Sala Thanassi

Copyright © Naomi Kinsman
All rights reserved.

Printed in the USA
First Printing: December 2009
978-0-578-04487-3

A Society of Young
Inklings
Publication

Think left and think right and think low and think high. Oh, the things you can think up if only you try!

– Dr. Seuss

Table of Contents

Poetry

Foreword

The Inklings have outdone themselves again... Just wait until you read their short stories and poems! The Inklings Book 2009, our second annual anthology of work by young authors, features imaginative stories, thought-provoking poems, and also each author's unique perspective on the writing process.

In the interviews at the beginning of each chapter, you'll read about the journey each of these young authors traveled as they wrote and revised their stories. Revision, especially, is an important part of the writing process, because when writers revise they can build on their story's strengths and fix any weak spots. From each of these young authors, you'll learn about a specific revision strategy they used to help strengthen their story or poem. We encourage you to try some of these revision strategies as you polish your own writing.

At the Society of Young Inklings our goal is to inspire and encourage young writers, whether they've been writing for a very long time, or are just starting to dream about creating their own stories. We hope our Inklings Book 2009 will inspire you to write and revise stories of your own!

What is an Inkling? We're so glad you asked! Inklings are young writers, 1st grade through high school, who promise to:

- Write about what truly matters to us.

- Expect imperfection from first drafts... We use first drafts as clay from which to form final pieces.

- Play with words, experimenting until our stories are delicious.

- Curiously explore and observe the world because we know stories are in the details.

- Marinate ourselves in superb stories, learning from master storytellers.

- Share our writing with others.

- Write. We do not just think about writing!

- Encourage other Inklings.

- Continually strive to become better writers.

We hope you'll join us! You can learn more about The Society of Young Inklings at www.younginklings.com.

Create pictures in a reader's mind

One of the most satisfying parts of being an author is hearing readers describe scenes from your story as though they actually saw, heard, and smelled them.

After completing *Priya's Adventures*, Amrita Bhasin read her story aloud and found moments where she could add details about how a moment felt, sounded, looked, smelled or tasted.

As you read, pay attention to how the descriptive details make Amrita's scenes come alive.

Amrita Bhasin

Amrita Bhasin, a 3rd grader, has always had a passion for reading adventure books. Her story was developed with some ideas from her younger brother. Amrita's hobbies include art and playing sports. Her favorite sport is field hockey. Her dad is a coach so she never gets in trouble! She enjoys a variety of foods and all of her stories have some focus on food. When she's older, Amrita wants to be an author or an artist. She would like to be an author because she believes that in an imagined world anything is possible and you can use crazy, strange and mysterious ideas in your stories!!

Here are some of Amrita's thoughts on the writing and revision of *Priya's Adventures*.

What is your process for writing a story?

First I plan, then draft, revise, edit and publish. I always share my stories with friends and family. Sharing is important because you can get ideas from other people and they can help you make your story better.

What is your favorite part of your story?

My favorite part of the story was the witch and all of her rhymes, like "Ickity Bickety." I had a lot of fun making up the rhymes.

You experimented with adding descriptive details that would make pictures in a reader's mind. How did you know which details to include in your final story?

> I really zoomed in on the story and made the reader picture what was happening. Like in the underwater sea party, I made up all the sea creatures and their roles in the orchestra.

What advice would you give other Inklings who want to write fantasy stories?

> Take an old story that you once read or wrote that you think is interesting, add lots of details, change some parts and make the story better. Add magic. Use ideas from your imagination. Be creative. Sometimes I keep ideas in my head for a long time before I use them. For instance, the castle in this story was an idea I had in my mind and I decided to use it in this story.

Do you have any other advice for young writers?

> Last year my school librarian gave me a book with a poem in it that said something like, "If you have an idea, don't forget it, just write it down on a piece of paper. Later you can make it into a story. "Ever since I read the poem, I always keep a pad of paper in my car in case I get a sudden idea.

Priya's Adventures

by Amrita Bhasin

CHAPTER ONE

Yali

Priya was a little girl who really longed for an exciting adventure. She wanted an adventure because she didn't have a brother or sister to play with. She only had a fish who she thought was boring. She always carried a secret map in the left pocket of her dress, in case she ever got lost or found herself on an adventure.

One evening as she was sleeping, she was suddenly awoken by a creaky noise. She wondered what the noise was. Then, something under her pillow started poking her. It was a key with a star on the end.

Suddenly out of nowhere, a magical door appeared. She heard two little voices inside.

One said, "Priya, what are you doing?"

The other said, "Go ahead, try it. You're in for an adventure." Priya thought for a moment and agreed with the second voice.

She put the key in the odd looking lock. It was in the shape of a butterfly. The door opened. She picked up a lantern that was lying on the floor and walked inside.

What a strange place! Priya thought. She tiptoed quietly down a long passage that seemed to be leading somewhere. It was dark and dusty. In an instant, a cloud of dust blew the lantern out. Far down in the distance, Priya saw a passageway that was glowing. She went through it.

An odd looking and rather small dwarflike creature blocked her way. He had wild purple hair. Priya was at first a little frightened but them she noticed that the little creature had tears running down his face.

"Are you ok? What's your name?" she asked.

The creature said in a small and shy voice, "My name is Yali. I was collecting berries in the forest with my mother. There was a storm and I got separated from her. My mother always said that if I was ever lost, I should stay where I was. So I have been waiting in this cave but I don't know where she is....." At this, Yali started sobbing.

Priya was a kind girl so she responded, "Don't worry, I will help you."

Then she led Yali further down the passage.

"Do you know the way out of here?" she asked Yali.

"No, not really," mumbled a shivering Yali.

"Well, I just got here so I don't know the way either," Priya said.

CHAPTER TWO
Fairyland

Priya and Yali tried different passages but none seemed right. Then Yali had an idea. He went down one passage and returned with a bundle of sticks.

"What are those for?" Priya asked.

"Well, we could use one stick for each passage. That way we will know which passage we tried and which we did not."

So they went around placing sticks in every passage. Finally they tried one really scary looking passage at the end of which there was a long cave with a very small hole.

Priya and Yali tried their best to push each other through the hole. The the two companions saw a foot hole in the rough dirt. So they took turns putting their feet in the foot hole and pushed themselves through the opening.

When they went through the hole, they found themselves in a bright and grassy meadow. Priya saw tiny figures who were much smaller than Yali. Priya and Yali could both tell they were fairies because they had wings and garlands of flowers around their necks. Through the open window of a small house, they could see a mother fairy putting bread into an oven for her children. The mother fairy gestured to them to come in and eat fresh-baked, just-out-of the oven bread. They accepted the invite and came in and drank orange juice and freshly baked bread with butter.

They said, "Thank you," to the fairy who unfortunately couldn't understand what they were saying. They had to find out where they were.

Priya asked one of the fairies who was skipping by, "What kind of place is this?"

The fairy simply shook her head with no response.

Then Yali saw a sign on a post, written in a language he could not read. *Very strange!* he thought to himself.

CHAPTER THREE
The Underwater Party

Priya remembered her secret map. She took it out and unfolded it. As she looked over the zigzag lines on the map, she noticed in one corner in tiny writing the words, *If you ever end up in fairy land, just say these words: "Please, may I be back in a whale's eye."*

As soon as Priya uttered this sentence, she and Yali were transformed into mermaids and around them was a shining blue sea.

A sea turtle approached them and soon they had made friends with him.. The sea turtle showed them around and then said that he was heading to an underwater party and invited them to join him. There would be music and dancing and some yummy treats, he told them.. Priya and Yali gladly accepted his invitation, because they were in a really good mood for a party and hungry. They swam to the ocean floor and joined the party.

At the party there were all kinds of sea creatures. A crab was hopping happily, making click-clack sounds with his claws and conducting an orchestra of sea creatures. A fish darted around drumming its tail against a rock. Three whales swam in a large circle around the party, humming and singing. A group of sea horses held hands and danced in the middle. An octopus held a maraca in one hand, a tambourine in another, a saxophone in a third, a horn in a fourth, a flute in a fifth, a clarinet in a sixth, a xylophone in a seventh and a harmonica in his eighth hand. Two baby dolphins turned somersaults and everybody seemed to be having a wonderful time. It was quite an amazing sight. Yali joined excitedly in a funky dance with Priya.

A mother dolphin asked Priya if she would like something to eat. She led Priya and Yali to a table with a delicious-looking feast. There were jellyfish rolls, seaweed rice cakes, sea-sponge pies and other wonderful dishes that Priya had never seen before. Priya and Yali tasted a little bit of everything.

After they'd had enough, Priya and Yali thanked the considerate dolphin and the other sea creatures. The sea turtle led them both to the surface of the water where they thanked him and said goodbye.

CHAPTER FOUR
The New Friend

Once they were back on land, Priya saw a castle on a hill in the distance. They hiked up the hill and knocked on the castle door. It was opened by a young boy who looked no older than Priya. He said that his name was Raj and invited them in.

Since Priya and Yali were both dripping wet from their underwater adventure, he first led them to a guest room in the castle and brought them dry clothes to change into. After this he took them to meet his mother and introduced them both as his new friends. Raj's mother said that they could stay as long as they wanted and join the family for dinner later.

Raj took them for a tour of the castle. Then they sat in his room and played some board games and cards. They were enjoying their play so much that they didn't notice that it was almost dinner time.

Raj's mother called them down for dinner. Dinner was a spectacular meal consisting of rotisserie chicken, French baguette, roasted vegetables, potatoes and fruit salad. Dessert followed which was a freshly baked apple pie.

After dinner, Raj showed them to guest rooms where they changed and got into bed. Priya was tired from the day's events and slept very soundly.

The next morning Priya and Yali got ready and after a hearty breakfast prepared by Raj's mother, they were ready to say goodbye and set out on their way.

"Can I come with you?" asked Raj.

Priya and Yali put their heads together and after a moment of discussion they decided to let Raj join them as a companion. Raj's mother said it was ok with her as long as he was back by bedtime. She packed them some food for their journey and the three travelers set off on their way.

CHAPTER FIVE
The Scroll

Priya, Raj and Yali walked until they came to a river. They were tired so they sat by the river to rest for a while. The water in the river was crystal clear. Suddenly Priya remembered the spell she had spoken the day before.

She took out her map and explained their adventure. Raj was excited and curious about the underwater party. He wished he'd been with them.

Priya read the mysterious writing again "Please, may I be back in a whale's eye."

When she said this, a flash of light hit her eyes and she found herself sitting in a lovely garden under an apple tree with Yali beside her.

But Raj was nowhere to be seen.

Then they heard someone shouting, "Priya! Yali! Where are you?"

Priya and Yali walked towards the place the noise was coming from. All of a sudden, Priya slipped on something. When she picked it up, she saw that it was a paper scroll.

Priya unfolded the scroll and read it out loud. "*STOP! Danger lies ahead! Pick one way and stick with it. If you happen to go astray, you will end up in a thicket.*"

"How strange. What in the world could this mean?" Priya wondered.

"Well," said Yali, "I think there's danger ahead and we could end up in a thicket."

"But we don't want to end up in a thicket. We want to find Raj, don't we?" said Priya.

Suddenly they saw Raj running towards them. Out of breath, he told them what he had discovered.

"I... I saw a witch over there," he said pointing towards a forest.

"...You will end up in a thicket" said Priya repeating the words from the scroll. "A thicket is a kind of forest," she explained.

"What did the witch look like?" Priya asked Raj.

But before he could answer, they heard a singing sound from the forest. "Parsley, sage, rosemary and thyme. Once I've driven them all out, the forest will be mine."

"It's the witch!" whispered Yali in a scared voice.

CHAPTER SIX
The Witch

Priya, Raj and Yali walked softly to the edge of the forest. They tiptoed from tree to tree, hiding behind the tree trunks until they were close enough to see the witch. She was dressed in rags and her long dusty hair came all the way down to the ground. She wore a big pointy torn hat. Her long crooked nose hung down over her face. A small black cat sat on her shoulder nibbling at her rags. She had a big black cauldron on a fire. She was stirring the contents like crazy.

"Twigs, leaves, dead snails. Flower petals, bugs, squirrel tails. Ickety Bickety Calamazoo! Once I have the forest, la la loo!" she sang.

The witch herself was eating Turkish Delight. It was quite a scene.

"What if she spots us?" whispered Raj.

All of a sudden the singing stopped and the witch looked around.

"Hush," whispered Priya, "I think the witch has sensed that we're here."

"Come out my little cuties. Come out wherever you are." The witch sang in a wicked voice.

"We need to find a place to hide," said Yali anxiously.

By now the witch had started to wander around the forest looking for whoever was in her forest.

"Quick! That tree," instructed Yali. "Wait, let's think of a plan," said Priya. So the three of them put their heads together and thought of a plan.

Priya climbed up a tree with strangely shaped branches. Raj waited at the edge of the forest so if the witch ran he could grab her, and Yali followed the witch. They were ready. Yali grabbed the witch's magic wand and threw it up to Priya.

Priya aimed the wand at the witch's back and yelled at the top of her lungs, "Ready... Aim... Fire."

CHAPTER SEVEN
All a Dream

Someone was shaking Priya.

"The w... witch. Yali! Raj!" muttered Priya.

She was now sitting up on her bed. She opened her eyes and her teddy bear was lying by her side.

"What's going on?" asked Simrin, Priya's cousin who was visiting from India.

Priya told Simrin all about her adventure.

That's such an interesting dream. I think you should write it down in a book before you forget it." said Simrin.

"But, it wasn't a dream. It was real." said Priya.

"Priya, it was a dream. Remember you fell asleep while we were sitting on your bed reading 'Alice in Wonderland'," said Simrin.

Priya had to agree. But in her mind it was as though it had all really happened. And, she thought she would never forget her amazing adventure with Yali and Raj.

The End

Discover a Character's Wish

Stories are moved forward by characters who have a significant desire and take action to make that desire, or wish, come true.

After completing *Redwing*, Sala Thanassi thought about each of her characters, what they wished for, and what they did in the story to achieve their desires. Then, she added details and actions that would help make those wishes more clear to her readers.

As you read, notice Sala's strong characters and the actions they take to make their wishes come true.

Sala Thanassi

Sala Thanassi is nine years old and in fourth grade. Aside from reading and writing, she enjoys playing basketball and soccer, drawing and going to the movies. Her favorite books are Pendragon, Shadow Children, and Matilda. She lives in Portola Valley, CA. She likes playing on the piano, and when she goes into fifth grade she will play the saxophone. After school she does singing, cooking and ceramics.

Here are some of Sala's thoughts on the writing and revision of *Redwing*.

What do you like most about writing?

I like writing because in your book, it's all up to you. The characters, their personalities, the settings, etc. You can make up anything, such as a giant evil flying rabbit. It's just nice to be in my very own world.

What gave you the idea for *Redwing*?

Well, it was actually two things. One is, when I went to Seattle I was in this art class. I made a picture of a small colorful bird, and

later I thought, why not make a story about a bird? And two is, a friend of mine, Tori Rarick, was always writing stories about animals, and she seemed to enjoy it a lot. So I thought it might be a nice change.

During your revision, you worked on highlighting the change in your characters throughout the story. How did you choose what to change in your story?

With a tiny bit of help by my mom, we sat around and thought about the characters and took notes, and then later I added them into the story.

What advice would you give to other Inklings who are working on adventure stories?

When you are writing a story, don't make it too confusing. Really think about your characters, and what they want. Also, when I write a story, if my character is talking, for example, I try to avoid using common words such as, "I like that," Sarah said. Instead, I write, "I like that," Sarah exclaimed. That really helps me.

Redwing

by

Sala Thanassi

34

The jungle twittered and chirped as Redwing folded his wings. His black eyes were open wide and darting around as he listened for any signs of the Citrus. Suddenly Redwing heard a loud rrreeeeap! The Citrus! With a big heave Redwing swung off the purple branch and opened his wings.

Soon he was soaring through the emerald-colored treetops, his beak clucking nervously. Today was the day a new member was going to be assigned to the Citrus, and everyone had to be at their best. Earlier that day Redwing had pruned his feathers and checked his rainbow-colored wings to make sure he was in perfect shape. Twwannng! Twwanngg!

The newcomer had arrived.

Silence. That was all Redwing heard as he gazed into the small clearing where the new bird was to be escorted. Now that he had time to think, he had time to focus on the Citrus, the very important birds that were in charge of the flock. The main leader was a huge bald eagle with tiny eyes and a mean posture. You don't want to mess with him.

There was a twitter, and Redwing looked up eagerly. Sure enough, a handsome Cardinal with bright red feathers and a red chest emerged. He had sharp little claws and a pointed beak, perfect for cracking open nuts and slicing berries. Redwing glanced around and saw that several doves were admiring him.

"Hello everyone," the Cardinal chirped, which brought Redwing back to his senses.

"My name is Twig, and I am very proud to be part of this... er... Citrus," he continued, "It is a very big honor. It makes me feel as if I am important, just like you." He puffed out his chest. "Sometimes I will wonder if I matter in this world, and then I will say, 'Of course, I am now part of the Citrus!'"

The clearing paused... Then there was a thundering sound of five hundred claws being sharpened on wood. That applause caused Twig to look a little sheepish, as if he wasn't used to that much attention. Personally, Redwing thought that he was a little full of himself.

A tiny yellow chickadee escorted him to the branch he would rest on. She led him all the way through the formal birds, past the cooing doves, (which he smiled and winked at) and all the way to his bright blue branch, where Twig settled next to him.

"Hi," Twig said, in a slightly nervous tone of chirp.

Redwing ignored him.

"So, is it true that the Citrus was created a thousand years ago by birds called Bygons and that the forest is magical?" asked Twig.

"Mmm hmmm," muttered Redwing.

"... and that there is fabulous food and hot chicks?"

Redwing swung around and stared at him. This guy had some nerve! Suddenly Twig burst out laughing.

"I'm just kidding you, bro'! Y-you really fell for that!"

Redwing smiled nervously.

"Dude, I'm not that kind of guy. I'm really not. OK, I'm a little-" but he never got to finish his sentence because suddenly the leader of the flock sent out a piercing war call.

Redwing panicked. "What's going on here?" he stammered to a plump tree sparrow next to him.

"Hunters," she cried, "they're coming this way!"

He gasped and for a moment he was back in his nest, hearing those dreadful gunshot noises when he was only two, not aware that any second his life might go blank. Then there came another shot, accompanied by a loud crack! above him. He remembered turning his little head to look up and then feeling his stomach drop. The nest had plummeted toward the ground and Redwing had been badly injured. Ever since then he had been timid and terrified of hunters.

There came the warning shriek, although louder this time.

"Everyone move out!" the leader Foxspawn bellowed, and spread his wings.

There was a great flutter as hundreds of birds took flight. Twig was flustered.

"What's wrong?" he yelled above the chaos.

"We're being attacked!" Redwing screamed back, "Hunters are catching up to us!"

He just caught a look of surprise on Twig's face before Twig looked up and soared off the branch into the sky.

"Hey! Wait up!" Redwing cried.

In a second he was next to Twig, beating his wings furiously to keep up. The bright red cardinal soared effortlessly through the blue sky, much faster than expected. Redwing had always been the best at flying, and when he was young he had been the first to pass his flying test, but Twig was no match for him.

He's better than me at everything, Redwing thought.

Bang! Redwing glanced back to see a silver bullet rocket toward Twig.

"Incoming!" Redwing shrieked to him.

It turned out Twig didn't need his help, because he dodged it as easy as cake. It missed him by a yard. Redwing breathed a sigh of relief and flew closer to Twig. Even though he was a big show-off, he felt like a friend to Redwing. They flew in shocked silence, and occasionally Redwing glanced over to see that Twig's face was pale and sweaty.

What happened next was so fast that Redwing couldn't take it in quickly enough. One minute there was the sound of a gunshot, and

the next second everything turned black and Redwing was falling.

Down, down, down he went. Branches whipped at him from both sides, yet he didn't feel a thing. Redwing was barely aware that several of the flock were calling out to him, but he couldn't make out what they were saying.

"What was," he thought, "that whistling sound?"

He just became aware of the throbbing pain in his left wing when he hit the hard ground with a soft thud, and everything went black again.

Redwing's eyes opened a slit and he could barely make out Twig, hovering above-

Wait.

Twig. Twig came back for him? Why would he...

Snap. Crunch. Something was moving. Then a grasshopper dropped at his head and Redwing weakly picked it up with his beak.

"A little snack for you," said a voice that made Redwing start, "We don't want you to have low energy." It was Twig.

All through that day Twig took care of him. He fed him thoroughly and wrapped Redwing's wing in stiff brown leaves from the forest ground. A little later, he tried to get Redwing to fly, but when that didn't work he took some magical water from the spring, not far away, and dumped it on Redwing's injured wing.

The magical powers healed it quite efficiently so that Redwing was able to flap it a couple of times. All that time he was thinking about his dad, who had a scar on his left wing. His dad had been a great bird, everything a kid could ever want. One day, (Redwing was only six) he had gone out to get some food, and had disappeared. Ever since then Redwing had been really angry at the world and thought that everything was unfair.

Two days of being cared for and Redwing was ready. Redwing and Twig both flew up to the tree above them and looked out to the land beyond. The many twinkling lights on the treetops were sparkling beautifully.

"Come on," Twig urged him.

Redwing took a deep breath, and launched himself off the branch. As he flew, he looked down at the glimmering forest beneath him. The wind rushed through his feathers, making him close his eyes in joy.

They rested on a maple tree for the night. Before they went to bed, they talked a little. Redwing found out that Twig had a younger sister who was a total airhead. He couldn't stop laughing when Twig told him about the time she had jumped off a branch without looking and had landed in a pile of shriveled up banana peels. There was also the time that she "trimmed" her feathers and ended up nearly bald on

one side. Twig's parents were so worried that she might actually hurt herself that Twig was assigned to look after her day and night.

Before Redwing went to bed, he wondered what it would be like to have a sister of his own.

After a good night's sleep, Redwing thought he would go explore. He hopped along the dry, cracked wood, his claws catching on it. He almost stumbled over an acorn but caught his balance. After a while, Redwing came upon a clump of dry leaves resting on a tree branch. He curiously poked his head inside. Lying in the nest were two baby squirrels! Their wide eyes were darting around, and they kept twitching their noses nervously. A soft clicking sound came from behind Redwing. He twirled around, and instantly received a rock in the face.

"Ow!" Blinking dirt out of his eyes, Redwing looked up to see who his foe was.

Shielding his eyes with his strong wing, he looked up to see a black furry mound towering over him. It had big buck teeth and a bushy tail. The squirrel chucked another rock, but this time Redwing was too fast. It went sailing by him, so close that he felt the breeze ruffle his feathers.

"Who are you and what are you doing here?" said a gruff voice.

"Well," Redwing started, trying not to be nervous, "I'm Redwing, and I'm staying here for today, so I thought I might explore. Who are you?"

"Umm... Tar," muttered the squirrel uncomfortably. She tensed up again. "But what are you doing near my brothers?!"

Bewildered, Redwing stammered, "What... these are your brothers?"

Tar nodded, "Mom went out to collect nuts, and so she left me home with the boys. I was just going out to find some water and then I heard you."

Redwing nodded back and said, "Hey, do you want to come with Twig and me? We're going to look for the flock. I fell, and... well... we sort of lost them."

Tar looked around. "Sure," she said finally, "I saw the flock fly by here a couple days ago, maybe I could show you the way. I don't think mom would mind me leaving for a couple of days. But we have to take them." She jerked her head toward the nest. "I think they're old enough to come. They just learned to fly and are almost as fast as I am."

"WOW you are flying squirrels?" stammered Redwing.

Tar nodded enthusiastically.

They scurried down to find Twig. They found him at the base of the tree, collecting water.

"Twig!" Redwing called out. "I found someone to show us the way back." They jumped down next to Twig, and Redwing told him, "This is Tar and her little brothers. Tar, this is Twig."

"Cool, dude," Twig told Tar. Tar laughed sarcastically, "Actually, it's dude-ess." Twig laughed too.

"What, you mean you're a girl?"

Tar smiled, "Actually, yes," she told him. Twig stopped

laughing.

"So," he said, "you're really a girl?"

"Yep," Tar answered.

Twig was stunned, but after a while he closed his mouth and shrugged. "Fine by me," he answered.

"So, when do we leave?

The next day they all sat on the top branch of the tree, ready to take flight. Twig glanced over at Redwing.

"Ready?" he chirped.

"Ready," Redwing said.

"Ready," Tar announced.

"Ready," squeaked her little brothers. They all jumped up into the air. Redwing soared through the sky, Twig beside him, with Tar and her brothers leaping from tree to tree beneath them. Tar was helping them go home. They were going home.

As they skimmed the treetops, Redwing looked down at the land below. Something caught his eye. It was a splotch of brown. He thought it looked intriguing, so he dropped back.

He called to the others "Hey, um, I think I forgot something. You go ahead. I'll catch up."

Tar just shrugged, and they kept going. Redwing slowly descended, circling the trees. He heard a faint rustling sound, punctuated by a yelp. This made Redwing cautious, and he tried to make as little noise as possible.

When he landed, he saw a large robin with beautiful red plumage looking angrily down on a bird who was much bigger than he was, and an assortment of colors. Apparently he was unconscious, because he was silent and still and his eyes were closed. The robin looked up to see who had come, and when he saw Redwing, his eyes grew wide and confused.

He said to Redwing, "Who are you?"

Redwing told him.

The robin gasped, and stumbled backward. It was then that Redwing noticed the deep scar on his left wing. It felt like something punched him in the gut so hard it knocked him backward. He managed to choke out, "D-Dad? But..." and for thirty seconds, they stood staring at each other.

After he had gotten over his shock, Redwing said, "You've been gone so long...." Redwing was surprised at how calm he was.

His father replied, "Yes, but I ran into a little trouble," and he looked down at the rainbow bird lying at his claws. And then he spoke one, simple word; "Bygons."

Redwing looked at the bird, slowly letting the reality sink in... except now, he was more confused than ever. "But ..." he started slowly, "but aren't the Bygons, like ... gone?"

"Well," his dad said. "No. They weren't dead and gone, at least not all of them. You see..." He clucked his beak softly, and sighed. "Well, I guess you better sit down," he continued. "It's a long story."

"So it all starts when I went out to collect food for you and your mother. You remember that, I suppose? Well, I didn't get far before I felt a rough breeze on my feathers. I looked up and saw a giant whirl of wind heading toward me. I panicked of course.

I saw a hole in the ground that was just large enough for me to squeeze through. I dived for it, and managed to go into it just as a storm hit. I burrowed deeper and deeper, and it got darker and darker. Finally, I got through all of the dirt and rock and hit an underground cavern. I tumbled out, and that's when I heard voices. It sounded like someone was arguing.

I peered around a corner and saw two brightly-colored toucans, one with a long jagged scar running down from the middle of his eye to his beak. It looked like he had been in a fight. One of them caught sight of me and gestured me over. I went over to them, and they looked me up and down.

I can't say much else, but we became good friends over time. Of course I thought that you and you're mother were killed in the hurricane, so I didn't go back. I soon learned that the Bygons had wanted to go back at first, but there had been no way to get out. So the cavern eventually became their home, and they worked on ways to improve it.

Indeed it was marvelous; they chipped off all the parts of the cavern walls that might be sharp or dangerous, and they even had electricity! I was sent down a long, brightly-lit corridor and into a room with beautifully designed ceilings and floors. A quilted green bed, the color of moss was in one corner, there was a fiery red cushy chair in another: and there was a wooden table with maple tree chairs around it, and a vase of violet flowers on the table. On the right side of the wall there was a big box that looked sort of like a refrigerator, except it was filled with nuts and berries.

I stayed in there for about three days, and then they took me on a tour. First they led me into the nursery, where a cheerful-looking bluebird was caring for all sorts of toddlers. I remember this one scruffy-looking baby owl: on his first day he flew to the ceiling and refused to come down. He was a mischievous little thing, full of tricks. Well, some of the Bygons were bad; they wanted to get rid of the children and eventually the rest of the herd had to ward them off.

They had a little trouble, though, especially with this one, Brutus. Since he refused to be kind, he was assigned the task of digging the tunnel back up to the world we had all lost. This displeased him much, and he decided to fight. He went on a rampage, and many Bygons were injured or even killed. Some agreed with him and joined him, and soon he had a whole army of birds. One day I was going up through the tunnel, out to get water, and the hole caved in behind me. But Brutus here got out too.

I was devastated that I was cut off from my companions, because I felt like they were my only family, the only life I had was with them. I was clinging onto my life below, instead of looking up at the world around me. If I had looked up, maybe I would have found you."

Redwing stared at him, an idea forming in his head. Finally he spoke. "Dad, will you come with us? I mean, I've been so lonely without you, too."

His dad glanced down at Brutus, and then back at him. "Of

course" he declared, going over and rumpling Redwing's feathers. Redwing smiled, and a couple minutes later they were back in the air, together.

While they were flying, his dad said to Redwing, "You know, everything's perfect now."

And indeed it was.

The End

Choose
a point-of-view character

When we read a story, we slip into another world. By choosing a specific character who tells the story, writers give readers a lens through which to view the story. The reader often feels like they become that character as they read.

After completing *One Georgia Peach*, Suah Cheong chose one character who could tell her story best. She revised her story, making sure to let Peach tell the story exactly his way.

As you read, notice how Peach's personality comes through in the way *One Georgia Peach* is told.

Suah Cheong

Suah Cheong is a 7th grader in Austin, TX. She is on the school dance team and in the top band. Besides writing and reading, she enjoys playing her clarinet, listening to music, drawing, and talking to old friends. Some of her obsessions are Hello Kitty, funky desserts, and of course cute animals. Her friends call her Sushi (for how much of it she consumes) and Hello Suah (for how much she loves Hello Kitty).

Here are some of Suah's thoughts on the writing and revision of *One Georgia Peach*.

When did you first start writing?

I wasn't born my talent (writing). However my 2nd grade teacher, Mrs. Bindi Gill, was an expert at teaching the writing basics and showing students how to use their creativity. From this, I was inspired to write on a daily basis. In 2008, I improved my skills even more by becoming an Inkling and taking classes with Naomi. Even though I moved from California the following year, I am still constantly jotting stories down.

What gave you the idea for *One Georgia Peach?*

This idea began one spring day in 2008. I was basically hiding behind my tote bag at my first Inklings class. Naomi put a pink

spiral in my hands and told me to make brainstorming webs. Happy to do something I was comfortable with, I opened the spiral to the first clean page and spun away. After I jotted down ideas, she told me to write a story.

"How long?" I said.

"I've seen stories as short as a sentence, and ones as long as a Harry Potter book," she answered.

Trying not to be choppy or lengthy, I completed two pages of words that would later improve and grow.

In Fall 2009, I looked back at my pink notebook and reacted differently to everything. Some stories were corny while others were dull. I had a strong reaction to that one particular story though. Every time I read over a weird part, a chill would go down my spine. This gave me an urge to get back to it.

I started working my way up the revision pyramid taking tiny steps at a time. Before I knew it, this old creation of words was transformed into a published piece of writing

You were asked to revise your story thinking about point of view. Whose point of view did you choose? Why? What happened to your story when as you looked at the events through one characters eyes?

I chose Peach's point of view for this story. At first I thought about changing everything to first person, but realized that keeping the story in third person would add something funky and new to my story. As I looked through just Peach's eyes, I had to take out details that Peach didn't know, and be creative by replacing the unnecessary details with better ones. I didn't take out every part though. I made Peach look things up on the internet instead of him not knowing anything at all.

How would you explain point of view to other Inklings?

Point of view is something that can change your story completely. Think about *The Three Little Pigs*. If one of the pigs was the narrator, the story would be different than if the Wolf was the narrator. The Pig might say, "The Wolf huffed and puffed and blew my beautiful house down!" Whereas the Wolf could say, "I had this sudden urge to sneeze and it resulted in the pig's house getting ruined. It was an honest mistake." My story would've been entirely different if Veronica was the narrator instead of Peach.

What are your writing goals for the future?

I'm not too sure about my future, but I'm hoping to get a book of my own published and stay a Young Inkling for as long as I can. It really helps me with a lot of things like finding the time to write (I wouldn't be writing continuously if I wasn't one) and finding my mistakes. I also want to improve my writing and grammar skills.

One Georgia Peach

by

Suah Cheong

It might seem fantasy, but there was once an incredible dog living inside a computer with a flying car. He was the size of a paper clip which is convenient only for those of you who are inside a small environment. This dog spent his days fixing tangled wires, decayed semi-conductor chips, and other major problems inside the average computer. Without fellows like him, the world could not function properly.

This magical dog was doing his normal duties—fixing a computer slow-down—to be exact. Yes reader, there is no real point of putting together a story of a normal creature. But this story has an inexplicable purpose. Welcome to the miracle that changed this amazing dog's life for quite a long time.

At about three in the afternoon on an Indian summer day (according to the weatherman's website), the dog was interrupted by a strange sensation. Now, think about experiencing something for the very first time. Do you feel your adrenaline starting up? You are experiencing the same thing as our lovely dog, here. His ears automatically overlapped his eyes, while his front paws came directly over his ears. His back paws trembled but somehow led the dog to his magic convertible car.

Soon the sensation stopped. But when the dog returned to his normal position, everything changed. The world he was in now had detail and something inexplicable. The incredible dog could now sense his surroundings. He couldn't imagine all the things his new life contained. In addition, his body had gone through a lot of change. When he looked down, he saw a whole new dog. He no longer saw a tiny, useless body, but a plump body covered in short chocolate-colored fur. He started to examine his new body, not knowing what was up next.

This miracle happened to be a knock on a door, which to the dog, was glorious. He looked up from his "examining dance" to see what the noise was. He expected some kind of electronic device, or maybe another dog; however he saw two human eyes staring back at him and a jaw below the eyes that was completely out of place.

The human turned out to be a young boy in overall jeans, willing to care for the dog. He immediately skipped off with a smile on his face. Shortly, he came with a woman and supposedly her husband. The dog suspected them as the boy's parents. The woman called the boy's name. "David, are you sure you're responsible enough?"

David. So that was the boy's name. David replied with his mouth in a small, creaky voice. "I want doggie's name to be Peach". And that settled it. David was now the official owner of Peach.

Soon, Peach discovered that there was another world beyond the crammed room they were standing inside. David led Peach through the door and into another colorful room. "This is my room, Peach. We're going to live inside it." These simple words came out of his mouth, once again, in the same small voice.

David's room was painted baby blue and was filled with shiny, polished toys. Peach was definitely in luck—nobody likes living in a messy room. David's mother entered the room moments later; asking David to come with her to something Peach thought was called the pet store. Long thoughts skidded through Peach's mind as the trio loaded into the family Honda van. What would be in the pet store? Why were they going there? Peach hoped that it was another positive world.

The pet store, of course, was a wonderful surprise for Peach. There were many things called chew toys nicely placed on the isles. Peach also thought he smelled delicious treats. David and Peach were both shorter than David's mother, so the two munchkins were looking up the whole time.

They walked out of the pet store holding a plastic bag with toys and accessories for Peach. David had a cute grin on his face as they once again loaded the van. Peach was about to be dressed up in a navy blue sweater and a red collar with a matching leash. And David just knew that Peach would like his new chew toys.

The trio was greeted by David's dad. David ran into his arms as he shouted out notes of joy. Peach did the same, which had a whole different effect, but made the family giggle in unison. He brought the family closer together, which is what dogs normally don't do when they're meeting their new family.

After the "giggle fest", the family walked through the front door of their tidy home. Peach was dog-piled by his accessories and toys which made him show his teeth and widen his eyes with joy. Peach had never felt anything like this in his life. He also had something new to have pride in. Nothing is better than showing off your new collar to the other dogs.

David led Peach to his room as he described his family members. Apparently, Mom was a strict and serious person and Dad was goofy and silly. David was a little shy.

"Everybody always tells me I act like Mom- but that's just half of me. I think I'm an outgoing person and I get along well with others."

When David entered his room with Peach, another miracle shocked Peach. There was now a big blue bean bag in the room (probably for Peach) and a fuzzy rug was placed in the center of the carpet floor. Peach trotted over to the new furniture and sniffed it. This new world was a hundred times better than the old life that had disappeared in the room adjacent to this one.

The days passed by too fast. Before Peach knew it, a whole month had gone by. There were now beautiful autumn colors outside David's small bedroom window. David explained how the trees outside went through a growth process. In the winter the leaves were usually not on the trees at all. In the spring, new leaves would grow giving the tree a fresh start. Summer trees were in between spring leaves and autumn leaves, and autumn leaves were identical to the ones outside right now.

The one tree that really stood out to Peach was one that had a

bendy trunk and danced even when there wasn't a cool breeze passing by. That explanation would have to wait 'till later. David seemed to explain everything that Peach came across so there weren't very many things Peach didn't know.

Peach was startled by the noise David made while opening the bedroom's door.

"I'm home Peach! School was awesome today. A lady from the city museum came in to talk to us about wind. Now I know just about 20 facts about wind and what causes it!" David told Peach about the presentation at school just before.

You see, Peach and David had this teacher-student relationship. David would transfer his learning to Peach, giving the two of them minds filled with facts. . At school, David would learn amazing things from his 2nd grade teacher, Mrs. Linnehart, and then Peach would learn the same things from the wonderful teacher, David. Pretty soon, Peach's IQ started to rise faster than the leaves were going through their growth. Peach was now a fluent reader, a fast problem solver, an intelligent author and a creative artist.

Most stories you hear about intelligent dogs are number-related. There's one I've heard about a dog owner raising up number cards in front her dog and her dog barking the amount of times on the card. Amazing, right? But what if it was all a coincidence? Those cards could've really annoyed the dog, causing him to bark more and more. Maybe the scent of the cards was nasty.

However, Peach's story was not a coincidence at all. There was something about Peach's enthusiasm that made him listen to educational things. Once, Peach had been attracted to the sound of national news on David's Dad's TV. It was like he couldn't resist the sound of learning. Peach's skill was kept a secret until…

"(Heh Heh lough lough) Hello. My (nuh nuh ame) name (ih ih ss ss) is (Puh Puh each) Peach." One freezing winter day, Peach started repeating this phrase over and over again.

Every time he repeated the phrase, he got better at saying it. By the end of the day, Peach could say, "Hello. My name is Peach," fluently.

David was the first one to witness this. He was sitting at his desk in his bedroom with Peach, doing his homework when it occurred for the first time. David immediately reported this problem to his parents. Without finishing his homework, David left the house with his Mom to take Peach to the vet.

"Hey Peach! How are you? You can call me Doctor Barbin. Now, don't tease me about my east Texas accent!" Peach's doctor introduced herself in her overly-Texan accent and chuckled to herself. She grabbed her clipboard and started recording things on Peach's profile. "Save to memory." These robot words came out of Peach's mouth removing Doctor Barbin's concentration from the clipboard. "What! Save to memory?" The doctor screamed at her assistant, "Veronica! Come here with the MRI machine!"

Sadly, David and his folks were forced to leave for home. David exchanged goodbyes with Peach and glared at the office staff as he opened the door. Veronica rushed into the room with a funny looking machine and gently placed it on the small bed in the room. She entered

some kind of code—probably the code assigned to Peach—most likely to save the data to Peach's profile.

She carefully listened to Doctor Barbin's commands, "Scan his brain and the neurons near his paws! Then immediately send the test files to my account! Inform me as soon as the MRI machine screen says File 109874 MRI result received! Put the dog in his assigned cage number-109874- and put the cage in room 30B!"

Peach was uncomfortable during the scan. His whole body was shaking and the supportive pads on top of him were extremely itchy. The room was pitch-black and Veronica had replaced his leather collar with a plastic tag. To a dog, it's horrible when someone else takes away your badge of honor- especially if it's leather.

To his surprise, Peach woke up in a florescent lighted room—he guessed it was room 30B—in what the neighborhood canines call "the anti-happy cage" or "the depression cage" and sometimes even "the torture cage." He called out David's name, but only got the echo of his voice and a strange beeping sound in return. Before Peach knew it, Doctor Barbin opened the crisp white door of the ugly room and gave the hallway a quick glance. She slammed the door shut, locked it, and double checked the hallway through the window.

Doctor Barbin was holding a tray of injections.

Peach said in the most robotic tone he could make, "Doctor Barbin, You know it's against my will to take my DNA."

Peach wanted to scare the doctor as much as possible. Doctor Barbin picked up a needle labeled "Brain test" in silence and slowly crept closer to Peach.

All of a sudden she replied in a hushed tone," And it's against my will to be talking to a dog. I'm going to insert what I like to call my medical concoction into your head and take that brain power away from you."

She stabbed the needle into his scalp, making Peach fall asleep.

Remember that dancing tree mentioned earlier? That is the key element of this story. It's what Language Arts teachers call the resolution of a story. It turns out that the tree danced because it had transformed from Peach's flying car into a tree. It was a signal for Peach that his car was ready to take him back inside the computer. While Peach was asleep in room 30B, he had a dream about the tree turning back into his car. He was so focused on the dream that when he woke up, his car was in front of him. He hopped into the front seat and flew out of the vet's office. His car faded from the real world to a place where Peach would be most happy.

Peach was unbelievably back inside the computer. According to new websites… Peach was gone in David's world, but would still have a place in David's heart and family. Before Peach arrived, David's family didn't get together much. During his stay however, Peach had brought the family closer together. Doctor Barbin ended up getting some of Peach's DNA but never figured out how a dog could talk. Her plans were to make billions of dollars by inventing an injection for dogs to make them talk. All of her staff members quit their jobs and her patients' families asked for their pets' information back. Everyone abandoned The Pets Who Soar (Doctor Barbin's office) and she had a bad reputation across the whole nation.

On the other side, David's family got millions of dollars from TV channels and they were more famous than celebrities. David would always wake up to the noise of flashing cameras.

Peach was so happy that he'd made a difference in the world. He was also thankful that out of all the existing worlds, it was the computer in David's house that was given to him. After all, everyone loves to say, "Home sweet home."

The End

Stretch important scenes

One way to add suspense to a story is to stretch out the important, dramatic scenes. By adding dialogue, action and character thought, readers experience these scenes in slow-motion, detail-by-detail, much like they experience dramatic moments in real life.

After completing *Rainbow Falls*, Kaitlyn Penchina looked for the exciting moments she wanted to highlight. She then added dialogue and action to play up the drama and suspense in those scenes.

As you read, notice how Kaitlyn creates drama in the important scenes with dialogue and action.

Kaitlyn Penchina

Kaitlyn Penchina is in third grade. When she isn't writing in her bed or on the couch, she likes to draw or read. She also likes baking cookies, muffins and bread. When she grows up she wants to be a magician, librarian or a baker.

Here are some of Kaitlyn's thoughts on the writing and revision of *Rainbow Falls*.

How long have you liked to write?

Basically, since I've known how. I like to write fantasy about animals or mermaids because then you always have unanswered questions that you can answer with multiple stories afterward.

What gave you the idea for *Rainbow Falls*?

I was thinking of a book called Sophia, the Swan Fairy. The Swan Fairy was so interesting because she could sing so high she could crack ice and make people who had been mean be nice to

her. I decided I wanted a swan as the main character of my story. I didn't use magic powers for my swans, though, because I didn't want them to be able to fix everything too easily.

You worked on stretching out the dramatic scenes in your story. What do you think this did for your final version of *Rainbow Falls*?

It made the story more interesting. A reader who read the shorter story might wish it were longer. Now, with the stretched-out scenes, the story feels like it's just the right length.

What advice would you give other Inklings who want to write stories about animals?

Instead of having another animal as a bad guy, have something like a tornado that would happen no matter what. Then your hero has a whole lot more to stop in the story.

Rainbow Falls

by Kaitlyn Penchina

Once upon a time, by an enchanted pond, there was a swan named Sweeden. He lived under a sparkling waterfall. He was very lonely.

One day, he was taking his daily swim and he got very hungry. So he looked under water for algae and seaweed. He saw mackerel and tuna but still no algae. He looked under a rock and saw a sparkling golden box and on it was his long lost father's name! His lost father's name was Seddon.

"Wow!" he breathed. "This is amazing."

He looked inside. There nestled in the gleaming box were gems of all colors, shapes and sizes. There were Moonstone, Turquoise, Diamonds, Silver, Gold, Rubies, Iron, Topaz, Amethyst, Emerald, Granite, Sapphire, Aquamarine, Peridot, Bronze and Opals.

He decided to look for more of the jewels. Maybe some fell out! He was paddling around, his head under water, when suddenly he bumped into two swans who were swimming happily towards him.

"What are you doing with your head under water?" Stan asked Sweeden.

"Mmmp!" Sweeden mumbled, sticking his head out of the water.

"Yuck! That water doesn't taste good. I'm Sweeden."

The two swans introduced themselves as Stan and Sabrina. They were twins.

"We are trying to hide so we wouldn't be caught in that what-ever-you-call-it at the other end of the pond." said Sabrina.

"Net." Stan corrected. "Do you want to hide with us? We could be friends."

"Yes." Sweeden agreed.

One day, Stan asked where Sweeden's family was. When Sweeden told them he had no family, they said they wanted him to join their family. The twins pleaded and pleaded with their dad, but no luck.

"You have unthinkably gone mad. We have no more room for another swan in our family," their dad retorted.

"Aww." The twins said as they shrunk away from their father.

One week later, while admiring the jewels, Sweeden told Stan and Sabrina the story of his mother and father.

"I was just out of my egg when a hunter came and killed my mother. My dad leapt in front of me to protect me but the hunter was already out of sight. The next week the hunter came back and killed my father. Luckily, I fled and hid in the waterfall. And when the hunter came back, he didn't see me so he went away."

Just as Sweeden finished telling his story—swoosh! Stan and Sabrina were swept away with the current right into some duck traps.

"Ahh!" Sweeden screamed. "I see my mom and dad's killer. And now Sabrina and Stan have gotten caught too! I see the "most honorable hunter's" shoes! Oh no!!"

"That's right. And soon I'll get you!" the hunter bellowed.

"I've got you now," the hunter shouted.

But Sweeden rushed so fast, he and his pointed beak broke the net! Stan and Sabrina were free!

"Hooray," they shouted.

"Ugh!" the hunter grumbled.

The hunter swung his net over and over but he never caught Sweeden.

So Sweeden, Sabrina and Stan raced away back to Sweeden's house.

"You little rascals," the hunter yelled. "I'll get you next time."

"There will be no next time!" Sweeden yelled back.

"Yeah!" the twins agreed.

After that, Sweeden, Stan and Sabrina were the best of friends. Sweeden followed his friends to their house. Their family listened with awe to Stan and Sabrina's story.

"Wow!" they gasped.

"Wait!" Stan and Sabrina's dad cried. "If you're telling the truth, you can show me the net tomorrow, right?"

"Right!"

"I pronounce you an honorary Slack-Back family member," Stan and Sabrina's dad said.

"Yay!" they cried. "Yay!"

Sweeden blushed. He zoomed home, got the jewels and raced back.

"Let's celebrate," Sweeden said.

He showed the twins' family the jewels. And his new family partied 'til they couldn't anymore.

I'll get you next time still echoed in the children's minds. Sweeden thought, *I hope I never ever ever have to see him again.*

That may sound finished, but Sweeden knew it wasn't.

The End

(or is it?)

Add Drama to the Climax

Readers can't wait to get to the climax. Who can blame them? It's the most exciting part of the story! Since readers look forward to the climax, as writers, it's our job to give them the most dramatic, thrilling moment possible.

After completing *Three Cheers for Little Ears*, Natalie Gould stretched out her climactic moment, adding action and suspense. Just wait 'til you read it... You'll be on the edge of your seat!

As you read, notice the suspense and excellent storytelling throughout Natalie's story, and how that only adds to her exhilarating climax scene.

Natalie Gould

Natalie Gould, age 10, lives in California with her mom, dad, brother, hermit crabs, dog, and chickens. She enjoys reading, writing, and drawing. She is perfectly happy with the size of her ears.

Here are some of Natalie's thoughts on the writing and revision of *Three Cheers for Little Ears*.

How long have you been writing? When did you first decide that you liked writing?

I have been writing small stories that I never finished since kindergarten. It wasn't until 4th grade that I actually started writing stories that had an ending. Writing is around my 2nd favorite thing to do. My favorite thing to do is read. Because of that, little sentences that would be good in about 30 different books keep popping into my head.

Where did you get the inspiration for *Three Cheers for Little Ears*?

> I was looking at a bunch of pictures of animals trying to decide what animal to use in a story and I saw a bunny with giant ears. That's when I decided that my character's flaw would be the length of his ears. He would get laughed at, and then he would somehow save the day with his little ears.

You worked on stretching out your climax scene. How did you add suspense to the fight between the rabbits and the coyotes?

> I tried to make it like you were fighting next to Bon E. Rabid and I tried to describe the little things that would make the rabbits win or lose. I tried to do it in more detail.

Bon E. Rabid is a very unique character. What is one piece of advice that you would give to other Inklings about creating interesting characters?

> Make sure your main character has a flaw that makes him/her stand out and save the day. If he lives in the world of giants, make him tiny. If he lives in the land of laughing hyenas, make him too sad to laugh, that sort of thing.

Three Cheers for Little Ears

for

by

Natalie Gould

my name is Bon E. Rabid. I'm a bunny and I have a problem. I look like a dog.

From the neck down, I look like a normal bunny, but on my head...

My ears!

They are the problem.

They are TINY,

MINISCULE,

MICROSCOPIC!!

I wasn't always like this. When I was little, I had normal-sized ears for a little bunny. When time came for my ears to grow, they didn't. Ever since, I've been teased by the big bunnies in my town.

When I walk through town, I hear voices asking, "Who's _that_?" I thought this was a bunny town. Why is that dog living here?"

I hated my town.

I lay awake at night, wishing my ears were **BIG** so I'd finally fit in.

One night, when it was my turn to be on guard duty, I fell asleep and found myself face to face with **COYOTES!**

"Back down, coyotes," I yelled.

They fell over laughing.

"What's a runty dog like you doing telling us to back down?" they asked.

I thought of a plan.

"Let's fight," I said. "Winner gets the rabbits."

"Fight for the rabbits?" they laughed. "Sure, let's go."

"Wait, I need a week to train," I said.

"We'll give you one day," they said.

"Four," I said.

"Three. And that's our final offer."

"Okay, deal. See you in three days at midnight."

And the coyotes were gone.

I waited until the coyotes were out of earshot. And then I made an announcement.

"All right, you rabbits. I just saved your lives. Now you have to help me fight the coyotes."

We trained for the next two days. I was the coach.

On the third night, we hid in the bushes. Finally at midnight, the coyotes came back. "One, two," I counted under my breath.

"Three. **Attack!**"

We jumped at the coyotes, surprising them. It was a very weird battle, in which normally the coyotes would win, but this was our backyard, our home and we knew all the hiding places, plus we had pitchforks.

The battle went on and on, until everybody was tired.

Suddenly, I felt the leader coyote's breath on my throat; I could feel his claws closing in on my side as I desperately waved the pitchfork around. His claws were reaching towards my throat and, summoning the last teaspoon of power I had, I used my short little ears to poke him in the eye.

With the split second of hesitation he gave me, I took a piece of rope from my pocket and tied him up. I signaled the other rabbits to do the same. They put down their pitchforks and attacked the coyotes with the rope I tossed them.

I looked around and couldn't believe it—we had actually overpowered the coyotes.

I was a **hero**. I guess my small ears do come in handy.

"**Three cheers** for little ears!"

The End

Play with metaphors

Metaphors add texture to poems. Each metaphor layers on top of the next, creating a complete picture by the end of the poem. That's why poets play with their metaphors after completing a poem, choosing the images that best fit what they really mean to say.

After completing *Earth Sound*, Meg Maurer found that many of her poem's images had to do with performance and rhythm. She considered how each image in her poem added to the whole, working to make her poem's picture clear.

As you read, notice the surprising word combinations, intriguing verbs and strong nouns in Meg's poem.

Meg Maurer

Meg Maurer is eleven and in the seventh grade at her junior high school in Forest Lake, Minnesota. She LOVES to read, write, listen to music, draw, and collect perfume. She also skis, composes music on the piano, speaks Spanish, and watches NCIS every Tuesday night. She is inseparable from her cell phone, iPod, and laptop keyboard. Her favorite things to write are poems and short stories, and she is terrified of writer's block and spiders. Meg is over-the-top ecstatic about her poem being accepted into the Inklings Book 2009!

Here are some of Meg's thoughts on the writing and revision of *Earth Sound*.

When did you first start writing poems?

I first started writing poems about two years ago, in fifth grade. My teacher would always play really soft music, usually music by Enya, while we were working. If I finished early, I would grab a piece of paper and a pencil, sit at the table closest to the speakers and write down whatever the music made me feel like or whatever I thought the music would sound like if it was written with words. I think music is where all of my poems come from.

What gave you the idea for *Earth Sound*?

> Like I said, music. In band practice, I was reading over the lyrics to our next song, and a phrase that popped off the page was "stars were headlights of a man-made sky," and I struggled all day to keep it in my head until I could get home and write it down before I forgot about it. As I sat there looking at those words, and the cursor blinking on my computer screen, the rest of the words just fell out of my fingers and into the keyboard.

During your revision, you experimented with fitting your metaphors with the central image of the poem: being center stage in your own life. How did you decide what to keep and what to change?

> I had to read the poem through a couple times out loud, and imagine an audience listening. Wherever there was something that just didn't sound right, I had to find something that fit just right. Deciding what to keep and what to throw was the same. Wherever it didn't sound right, I had to find something that worked.

What advice do you have for other Inklings who are writing poems?

> Revise, revise, and revise! It's good to revise, and just because there's stuff that needs to be changed, it doesn't mean that your poem is bad. Not at all! Revising is the best you can do for your poem—the more times you revise, the better it gets. You can't ever be perfect, but revising will get you as close as you can.

Earth Sound

by

Meg Maurer

Today

The sun rises with a new beat

The streets shake with a new rhythm

You wander with a new tune

Clenched in your fist

Seeping through you

Leaving sparkling footprints of

Rainbow melodies

Everywhere you go

And Today,

You're under your own spotlight

DancingScreamingYellingSinging

To your own music

To the confident beat of this
Human-
You-
Earth-
-sound.

Tonight
The moon shines with an unforgettable melody
The stars
Are miniature spotlights
You are beneath them all
Center Stage,
Center World,
Filling you
Drenching you
With this Earth sound.

Create Scenes

Writing poetry is a fantastic way to express strong feelings and to explore important memories. Specific details help readers connect with those strong feelings.

After completing *My Brother and I*, Kit Sanderson explored two memories brought to mind by the images in her original poem. Her exploration turned into another poem, written in a more narrative style. Kit found that revision doesn't always mean changing an piece of writing, sometimes revision inspires a new creation altogether.

As you read, notice the strong details in Kit's poem.

Kit Sanderson

Kit Sanderson is a sixth grader. She's had many remarkable experiences in her life. When she was in France and was a flower girl, she thought water was in the bottom of a wine glass and drank it, only to find it was disgusting wine. She was gagging for 20 minutes. She lives with her mom, dad, and boring bunny, cat and dog. She likes pie.

Here are some of Kit's thoughts on the writing and revision of *My Brother and I*.

When did you start writing poetry?

I started writing poetry this year. I realized that I really liked poetry when my teacher, Ms. Brown, gave us a lot of poetry assignments. I realized that I had a good knack for narrative poetry and it didn't even have to be about my life. I actually did a book report in poem form and I got an A+ and I felt really proud of myself because almost nobody else had gotten full credit. I felt that it was good for me to write poetry because I've been through experiences like no one else has.

What gave you the inspiration for My Brother and I?

> I wanted to write something about my memories with my brother. I remembered some things that happened with my brother and that was enough because it brought out a whole new world of expressing my feelings in poetry. My brother was a huge inspiration because he brought lots of happiness into my life.

During your revision, you experimented with adding specifics to your poem. What did you try out? What did you decide to change? What did you decide to leave as written?

> I tried out two individual memories and they were both very special to me because even though my brother would pick me up daily and whirl me around, it was the one time before he died that made it special for me. I left everything that was in my original poem because I didn't know exactly how to put those big memories into a small poem such as My Brother and I. It was valuable to write out my memories because to remember those memories brought a whole new world to life and I have another poem now too.

What advice would you give to Inklings who are working on poems?

> Don't think about it too much otherwise it will turn out nothing like you started with. If you want to write poetry, it should just be free, not captured in a bottle like fireflies. It doesn't need to have structure.

My Brother and I

by

Kit Sanderson

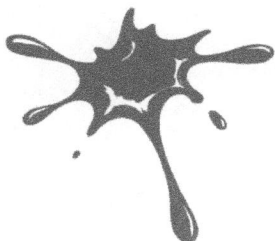

At two years old you'd think that I didn't know him
But no, I did
Very well in fact

He called me "Rose-Magose"
He'd pick me up and whirl me around
He carried me when need be
My Brother

He wanted to take care of me
He and I were inseparable,
The two of us wanted nothing more
Than each other's happiness

He told me that I was precious,

That I could never be replaced,

He told me he would never leave,

He was right

He didn't leave my heart

My Brother

He was scared to hold me

For with his huge hands

He could crush my soft spot

In an instant

He loved me more than

Any other

My Brother

Why did you leave our sight?

Why did you bother to show up?

Why do you make me blubber like this?

"I love you," he replied simply

"I love you too," I sob

I love him so much because he's

My brother, the brother who stands by my

Side when things are good and bad

He appears when things are

Not well, telling us

It's all right to be scared

He's there when times are fantastic too

Signifying that we couldn't be happier,

And that's my brother

Sean

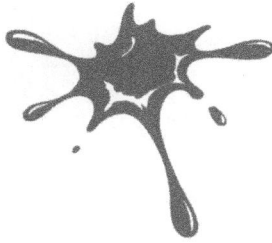

Experiment with Prose

Poetry, because of its short, concise format, allows writers to express a strong feeling or image. Yet, to find that strong feeling or image, it often helps to write about a poem's idea in prose, where you don't have to worry about word count.

After completing *Pessimist and Optimist*, Caleb Adderley wrote in long form about the ideas he'd begun with his earlier drafts. This process helped him discover and clarify the central idea of his poem.

As you read, notice Caleb's strong images and intriguing characters that play off of and build upon one another.

Caleb Adderley

Caleb Adderley, a sophomore homeschooler, has delighted in writing for several years. He first started in the model of his older sister. She has discontinued the art, but Caleb's got the bug for good. He writes when he can and tries to make sure he improves each time he sits down at his computer. When not writing, Caleb is very busy with musical theatre.

Here are some of Caleb's thoughts on the writing and revision of *Pessimist and Optimist*.

What inspired you to write *Pessimist and Optimist*?

This poem was inspired by desire to always be an optimist. I had just finished talking with someone who had a pessimistic viewpoint. I was determined never to be like that. Then I realized, that sometimes I'm the pessimist and they're the optimist. I had suddenly happened upon a dual nature of myself. I wrote the first draft of the poem, but as it was re-written, the revelation that these were both a part of me seemed less important than that my outlook on life is significantly affected by my faith.

How long have you been writing poetry?

I have tried to write poetry several times, rarely succeeding. I think this is the only poem I've ever really shared with anyone, outside my family.

As part of your revision, you experimented with writing in prose about this poem's ideas and images. What did writing about your poem in a different format do for the final version of your poem? Did you change any of your words or images? Why or why not?

This strategy helped immensely. It showed me that these two men could be deeper characters than I thought of at first; it even created an almost villain-hero relationship between them. I changed the entire poem because the new concept was much more interesting. It took a lot of work and some parent consultation, but in the end, I think the second draft is far better than the first. It has more interesting imagery.

What advice do you have for other Inklings who are writing poems?

Be sure that you're writing with a purpose. Poetry can be light-hearted, even whimsical, but I think the best poetry is the kind that teaches the reader a valuable lesson.

Pessimist and Optimist

by

Caleb Adderley

A pessimist and optimist
Together they would walk
They'd stroll the land, take in the sights
Of pros and cons they'd talk.

One, of course, would see the bad
He hated almost all
He'd never dare or bear to hope.
His heart a twisted ball.

The other liked to see the light.
He chose to find the best
He'd search for good in every man
A kind heart filled his chest.

The topic came between them,
Of crashing rocks and waves
Pessimist said, "I hate them all;
They make too many caves."

The second smiled to himself
And clicked his tongue, "For shame
Brave men freely gave their lives,
This very beach to claim.

They fought the sea and death and pain
And sought to bring the light,
They triumphed as they landed here,
To make a new life right."

The two attended once a concert
 Where a harpist played
Pessimist whispered to his friend,
"I knew we should have stayed

At home away from all this noise!
Can't she hear she's flat?
She's botched up nearly every note;
One couldn't play worse than that!"

Optimist silenced him with a hand,
And gently whispered back,
"I rather think I like this song
Nothing seems to lack.

It reminds me of a hidden place
A lost, but peaceful spot
Or some kind word that once was spake
And has now been forgot."

While flipping through an ancient Text,
Both men read the Book.
Pessimist said, "O, what a pain,
See; look at this, just look!

These words are far too hard for me
I'd rather dump the lot
'Condemnation' what is that?"
His friend just said "You ought

Not give up quite so easily
This Letter is for you
A love Note that's for all of us
And every word rings true.

"Well surely something isn't good,
The earth is not pure jewel.
The world will come to a fatal end,
Find good in that, you fool!"

Optimist smiled and knew he'd won
For he knew the truth of what was planned.
"The world may stop and I may die,
But with the One I still shall stand.

After all, that's why He came,
To change this dark world's end.
Should little I, much less than He,
Not do the same, my friend."

Why Not
SPILL SOME INK YOURSELF?

SPILLED INK
WRITING MACHINE

WRITER

Dive into SPILLED INK,
the Society of Young Inklings Official
Writers' Notebook, and every day becomes
a new opportunity for creative thinking and fun.

Both whimsical and practical, SPILLED INK is
filled with the inspiration, tools and tips needed
to develop the writing skills of fledgling authors
of all ages. Learn the writerly habit of attention to
detail; discovering and collecting ideas from everyday
experience that shape the characters, plots, settings and
details of fully realized stories. Learn to identify what
makes a good story by reading like a writer.
And record it all in SPILLED INK.

JOIN US
ON THE
ADVENTURE.

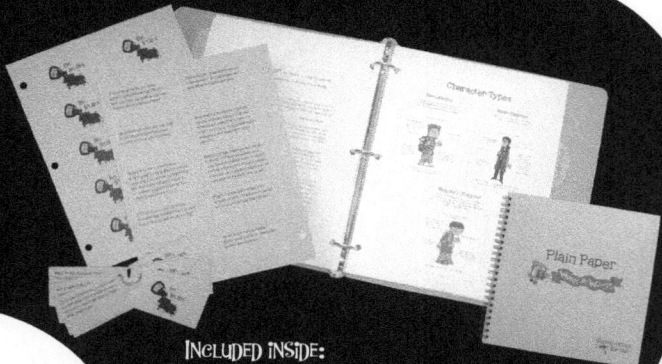

Character Types

Plain Paper

INCLUDED INSIDE:

30 cut-apart Ink Splats - playful, thought provoking
cards that help when you're stuck for ideas.

An official Society of Young Inklings mechanical
pencil

Plain Paper - a special Spilled Ink ruled notebook for
your writing adventures!

ALL CONTAINED
IN A STURDY, CLOSEABLE
BINDER POCKET.

2009 GOLD MEDAL WINNER
CELEBRATING YOUTHFUL CURIOSITY, DISCOVERY AND LEARNING THROUGH BOOKS AND READING.

Moonbeam
Children's
Book Awards

EDUCATIONAL/ACTIVITY BOOK

ORDER YOUR COPY TODAY AT
WWW.YOUNGINKLINGS.COM

Join the Inklings and submit your writing for next year's Inklings Book!

WANTED

exceptional stories and poems by young authors ages 8 - 18

FOR

Inklings Book 2010

Submission Guidelines at www.younginklings.com

The Society of Young Inklings is looking for tellers of tales and imaginative inventors... Join us and adventure through the world of words!

Here's the scoop. As a member of The Society of Young Inklings, you will receive the Inklings Membership Kit which includes:

An official Membership Certificate

Inklings emails with tips and encouragement

A paper copy of the Idea Files, our ezine

An official Inklings Decoder Dial

An Inklings sticker

An Inklings Bag Tag

Plus official Inklings have the opportunity to submit writing for our yearly publishing opportunity--The Inklings Book.

There is a yearly membership fee of $20. Teachers, email info@younginklings.com for classroom membership options.

www.ingramcontent.com/pod-product-compliance
Lightning Source LLC
Chambersburg PA
CBHW032008040426
42448CB00006B/533